HELP!

by Gabby Pritchard
illustrated by Jon Stuart

Institute of Education

Lizard went from rock to rock.

He saw some bugs.

'Yum, yum.
I like eating bugs,'
said Lizard.

Lizard saw some flies.

4

'Yum, yum', he said.

'I like eating flies.'

A ladybird went by.

'Yum, yum,' said Lizard.
'I like eating ladybirds.'

7

But Lizard was too fat.

The ladybird got away.

'Help me,' said Lizard.
'I'm stuck in the rocks!'

10

The ladybird looked at Lizard.

'I will help you,' she said.
'But you can not eat me.'

'I will not eat you,' said Lizard.

'Then I will help you get out
from the rocks,' said the ladybird.

The ladybird sang to Lizard.

Lizard went to sleep.

He did not eat all night.

'Look,' said Lizard. I can get out.

I am not too fat.

14

'Thank you,' said Lizard.

Teaching notes written by Sue Bodman and Glen Franklin

Using this book

Developing reading comprehension

Lizard likes eating bugs and insects. He eats too much and gets stuck between two rocks. Luckily, a ladybird is able to soothe him to sleep and when he wakes up, his stomach has shrunk sufficiently to escape.

This colourfully-illustrated story has a problem and resolution structure. One-to-one correspondence and left-to-right tracking need to be well established, as text appears on both pages and varies in its position on the page to support the story events.

Grammar and sentence structure

- Some repetition of phrase patterns, but greater variation of sentence structure than in Red band.
- Punctuation, including the use of exclamation marks and speech marks, supports phrased and fluent reading.
- Familiar oral language structures.

Word meaning and spelling

- Opportunity to rehearse a wide range of known high frequency words.
- Practise and consolidation of reading decodable words.
- Use of inflections 'ing' and 'ed'.

Curriculum links

Music – The ladybird sang Lizard to sleep. Learn some lullabies in common use and talk about how the sounds, the melody and the words sooth the listener to sleep.

Science and nature – Use non-fiction books and websites to explore the creatures that lizards like to eat. This work could be displayed with captions created by the children.

Learning Outcomes

Children can:

- read aloud using the context, sentence structure and sight vocabulary to read with expression and for meaning
- attempt new words in more challenging texts using their phonic knowledge
- comment on the events and characters in the story, making imaginative links to their own experience.

A guided reading lesson

Book Introduction

Give each child a book and read the title. Ask them to look at the cover and say who they think is saying 'Help!'

Orientation

Give a brief overview of the book, using the verb in the same form as it is in text. Say: *Lizard liked eating. He looked for things to eat. He ate too much and got into some difficulties.*

Preparation

Page 2: Say: *'Lizard went from rock to rock.' 'rock to rock'. Find that part. Think about the letters you would expect to see. He saw something good to eat. Can you find them in the picture? What are they? Let's check.* Model checking the text: *'He saw some ....' Read slowly through the word. Yes that's right. He saw some bugs.*

Page 3: *He caught one and ate it. He says something that helps us understand how much he likes eating. Find that part and read slowly through the word.* Model stretching the phonemes to slowly articulate the word. /y/ /u/ /m/ - *yes 'Yum, yum.'*

Page 4: Support the children to check letter information with picture information: *What did he see next? I see /f/*